© 2025 Demetrius C. Leonard. All rights reserved.

Copyright registration pending with the U.S. Copyright Office.
All rights reserved. No part of this book may be reproduced, distributed, or transmitted in any form or by any means, including photocopying, recording, or other electronic or mechanical methods, without the prior written permission of the author, except in the case of brief quotations embodied in critical reviews and specific other non-commercial uses permitted by copyright law.

This is a work of poetry. Names, characters, places, and incidents are products of the author's imagination or used fictitiously.
Any resemblance to actual events, locales, or persons, living or dead, is purely coincidental.

First Edition — 2025 volume 1

Copyright: Pending

ISBN: 979-8-218-86500-9

For permission requests, contact:

Demetrius C. Leonard

Email: Dcleonard732@gmail.com

Cover design by Robert Jarocki

Printed in the United States of America

DEDICATION

For Anny, *who first inspired me in 1996*
to turn fleeting thoughts and dreams into poems.
Your spark lives on in every word.
Deme, The Poet and Dream Master

"Since 1996, fleeting thoughts and dreams have taken shape in poems a timeless echo of the heart, captured at last in words."

DTP

ACKNOWLEDGMENT

This book of poems is lovingly dedicated to a dear friend from years ago— *Anny,* thank you for the inspiration that first lit my path in 1996.

Your insight, and the books you gave me to capture
my fleeting thoughts and dreams

helped transform them into poems that now find their place upon these pages. What began in 1996 has at last been brought to life, and the visions I held then are finally shared with the world.

Wherever you are, I hope you will one day hold a copy in your hands and know the spark you gave has never faded.

With much love,

Deme — *The Poet and Dream Master*

CONTENTS

Alexander: The Just King (A Dream-Poem in Ten Visions) 1
I. The Wanderer's Quest 2
II. The Kingdom Found 3
III. Laws of Justice 4
IV. Forging the Army 5
V. Growth and Prosperity 6
VI. Shadows of Opposition 7
VII. The Foiled Coup 8
VIII. A King's Burden 9
IX. The Golden Years 10
X. The Legacy of Justice 11
Aliens Attack Job 12
Brooklyn Smoke and Mirrors 14
Phenindione Dream 16
Gideon in the Church 19
A Senator's Past 21
The Silent Knight: Jay's Undercover Run 24
Destined by Love 28
Lines in the Sand 31
The Woman of My Dreams 33
The Knight's Vow 36
Work 38
Strength in the Fields 40
Leadership 42
When We Finally Meet 44
My Heart Remembers You 46

How Do You Feel About Me 48
A Plea for Understanding 50
Rich in My Dreams 52
Happy Valentine's Day 55
The Gift 57
Wheat.. 59
A New Day 61
Apart 63
Confession in the Moonlight 65
Hollow Remains 68
Kindling the Dawn 69
In the Colors of Love... 70
What Do I Want? 71
I See You... 72
The Second Half 73
Lovely Bride 74
Beyond Pigment 75
The greatest Love 77
A Garden of the Loves I Miss 79
Keep Hope Alive 81
I Will Not Fall.. 83
Gods hand 84
A Love I Pray to Keep 86
Eruption of Desire 88
To make you sigh 89
Dear John 91
The Auction of Shadows 92
The Estate of Night (Ode to E.A. Poe) 95
Paradise by the Sea 98

Dream of Us 100
Lightning's Gift 102
Free Will 103
Ghost in the Cabinet 105
In The Dream 108

Acknowledgment 110
Notes on Selected Poems 111
"The Auction of Shadows" 111
"Ode to E. A. Poe" 111
"The Woman of My Dreams" 112

About the Author – Demetrius "The Poet and Dream Master" ... 113
My Journey and Future Works 114

Alexander: The Just King
(A Dream-Poem in Ten Visions)

Prologue — 1997

I fell asleep and found a road.

made from moonlight and old vows, and there he was,

then the dream folded into a story.

a young man with restless eyes,

carrying a crown that hadn't been earned yet,

only imagined.

I. The Wanderer's Quest

Once upon a time, beneath a restless sky,
A young man walked with purpose in his eye.
He sought a throne, but not for vain display.
A realm where truth could guide the typical day.

Through months of road, through storm,
through dust, through night,
He carried visions stitched with what was right.
"My kingdom must be fair," his spirit cried,
Where peace is built with justice as its guide."
At last, the wind grew still, the clouds grew thin.
And beauty waited where his dreams begin.

II. The Kingdom Found

After long miles, he climbed a rising hill,
And saw a land that made the world stand still.
Rich fields rolled out like emeralds in the sun,
With rivers bright that promised more to come.

The people watched, both curious and wary.
For crowns had harmed them, heavy, cold, and scary.
Yet Alexander stood with open hands,
Not claiming hearts by force, but by his plans.

He chose that place where hope touched down
and vowed to build his future on hallowed ground.

III. Laws of Justice

"A realm without its laws will never last,"
He said, for peace is fragile, swift, and fast.
He raised courts where fairness could be heard,
Where truth was honored and not bought with words.

He chose wise judges, steady, calm, and clean,
To rule the grey where right was rarely seen.

Disputes arrived like thunder in the square.
He settled them with balance, firm and fair.
And soon the people whispered, bright with trust:
This king is just... his judgment isn't dust.

IV. Forging the Army

"To keep the peace, we must be strong," he swore,
"For danger always listens at the door."
He called the brave, the loyal, and the true,
And trained their hands to know what honor they knew.

Not cruel in might, not reckless in their pride
He taught restraint, with justice as their guide.
He walked their ranks, his courage close at hand,
and earned their faith like iron earns its brand.

But far beyond, in jealous courts and halls,
He heard the rumor: envy slowly crawls.

V. Growth and Prosperity

The kingdom bloomed like springtime after rain,
And joy ran wild through field and market lane.
Trade filled the roads, and harvest crowned the year,
New towns arose where doubt had lived in fear.

He built farms and schools with open doors,
Where minds could sail to wider, brighter shores.
The people laughed and praised his steady reign.
For under him, their labor wasn't in pain.

Yet in the dark, where rival whispers creep,
Discontent woke from its uneasy sleep.

VI. Shadows of Opposition

Where light burns bright, the shadows grow a spine,
and jealous hearts conspire in bitter wine.
Rival rulers schemed to stain his name,
and traitors within the walls fanned the flames.

So, Alexander listened, sharp and wise,
and built a net of watchful, silent eyes.
Not to spread fear, but guard the common good
To stop the knife before it drew blood on wood.

The air turned tense, the night grew cold and deep.
and rebellion stirred, then rose from troubled sleep.

VII. The Foiled Coup

The night of treason marched on whispering feet,
but dawn arrived, for betrayal to meet.
His watchers came with warnings,
straightforward and fast:
"They move tonight—this moment may be last."

Alexander stood, unshaken, sure,
With measured strength and mercy to endure.
He broke the plot before it could ignite,
And held the law like lanterns in the night.

Some faced his steel; some faced his mercy too.
And all who doubted learned what justice knew.

VIII. A King's Burden

A crown is gold, yet heavy in the mind,
A weight the cheering crowds will never find.
He walked alone in halls that echoed cold,
Where every choice was costly to behold.

To judge with truth yet keep compassion near.
To lead with strength yet never rule by fear.
In quiet hours, he wondered, almost torn:
Was he the dream… or was the dream reborn?

Still, he stood firm when doubt would test his flame,
and bore the burden like he bore his name.

IX. The Golden Years

His kingdom shone, a jewel nation praised,
A brightened realm that envy could not raze.
The borders held, the people lived secure,
The roads ran free; the fields were rich and pure.

Festivals rose with laughter, song, and art,
And knowledge found a home in every heart.
His wisdom spread like sunrise through the land,
and strangers spoke his name to understand.

Yet in his chest, a quieter thought drew near:
"What will remain when I am gone from here?"

X. The Legacy of Justice

Kings rise and fall; time has consistently shown.
Yet justice outlives marble, crown, and throne.
Alexander aged, yet laws endured long.
Laws were built to stand when men are gone.

When his last sunset softened into night,
The people mourned, then held his vision tight.
They taught their children fairness as a way,
and kept his courts as lanterns for the day.

Generations carried what he gave.
A living name no passing years could save:
Alexander, A Just King, forever brave.

— DTP

Aliens Attack Job

Monday morning coffee, keys, the office hum,
when the building shook as judgment had begun.
We looked outside; the sky went hard and gray.
A giant ship hung over town and blotted out the day.

Then chaos hit. The streets became a sprint,
Alien fire turned steel and stone to splint.
John, a coder, grabbed his laptop and ran.
Not with a weapon… just a desperate plan.

Across the road, a coffee shop—door tight,
Maria locked it fast against the night.

"Please," John gasped, and mercy won the fight;
She let him in, and they vanished from sight.

In the dark room, with sirens as their song,
John muttered, "Systems… even theirs go wrong."
He hunted signals, found a hidden seam
A crack in alien code, a human-sized dream.

They joined survivors, shared the doorway in,
Jammed alien channels, watched their ships begin
To stagger, fail, retreat into the haze, and
dawn returned to broken streets and dazed.

The city burned, but people wouldn't bend.
John rebuilt networks; Maria brewed again.
And from the wreckage—soft, unlikely, true
A new life rose... like morning breaking through.

— DTP

Brooklyn Smoke and Mirrors

In the dream, it started normally, just Brooklyn, just me,
Concrete veins and corner stores, that salty city by the sea.
Train rails singing overhead, bodegas, sirens, steam
Then one wrong turn of fate walked in and changed the dream.

A lawyer in a clean-cut suit with polished, practiced charm,
Spoken like he was safe, but I felt the quiet harm.
He smiled, and his handshake was smooth as silk,
Yet something in his eyes said, Kid, you're in it up to milk.

The cops rode by like kings of night, their lights a flashing grin,
But every glance felt purchased, like the city's stitched-on skin.
Politicians talked on podiums, "For Brooklyn! For the good!"
While deals were made in the dark, where truth was misunderstood.

An Indian man stood steady, calm, like he could read the air
Was he the bridge to justice… or a mask behind the glare?
In Brooklyn, even kindness had a price tag on the door,
And every "real one" carried secrets they were paid to store.

I tried to fade to ordinary, vanish in the crowd,
But Brooklyn pulled me closer, like thunder in a cloud.
Each block became a question, each corner felt like eyes
And trust turned into ash beneath those neon city skies.

So, I learned what dreams will teach you when they won't let you wake:
A badge can lie, a suit can steal, a smile can be a snake.
In Brooklyn, where the truth gets bent, then sold as something clean
Everybody's somebody… And nothing's what it seems.

— DTP

Phenindione Dream

In the dream, I held a borrowed kind of fire,
A cure-in-my-pocket, hope pulled taut like wire.
They called it Phenindione—locked behind the gate,
A guarded little answer that the world kept running late.

Twenty-five small cradles, twenty-five pale faces,
"Iron sickness," whispered prayers in hospital places.
And I couldn't stand the waiting, the paperwork, the pace
So, I stole what I believed was Mercy's missing piece of grace.

I bent my mind to a formula, no glory, no acclaim,
Just a desperate, quiet promise stitched to every name.
Not for money. Not for fame. Not to rise above,
I did it for a cause, I did it out of love.

But friends can turn to sirens when the fear gets loud,
They squealed, and truth wore shackles in a courtroom crowd.
The judge looked down like thunder, and the room held its breath,
and I stood there with my reasons, half-life, half-death.

"Yes," I said, "I did it. I broke the iron rule.
I crossed a line they drew, now bring me down if cruel.

But understand my hands: they shook, they weren't divine
I chose the babies' chance instead of toeing the line."
Then school became a battlefield of egos dressed as a gown,
My professor took corrections like a threat to his crown.
I proved him wrong academically, clean
He kicked me out for daring to be right where I had been.

Still, one mother listened with tired eyes, heart, brave,
I gave her what I had, the only hope I could save.
She took the formula for her child; no time to waste,
And when the baby strengthened, it rewrote the case.

I begged the other mothers, "Please let's do this right."
But fear spreads fast as rumor in the absence of light.
So back to court I went, with trembling, stubborn pride
To prove my cause was medicine, not reckless on the side.

At the strangest moment, the room began to shift left.
The academic crowd agreed this wasn't just a theft.
They weighed my work, my purpose, my intent,
and called it what it was: a rescue, badly bent.

The verdict wasn't spotless, but it opened the door

My name returned to school again, restored to what it bore.

And I woke up with that lesson still clinging to my skin:

Sometimes you do the right thing…

the wrong way…

And still, you have to answer for the sin.

— DTP

Gideon in the Church

Invited to church, though my Bible was thin,
I went for the truth, and I walked right in.
Natasha called on me, so I rose and said,
"What's life's true meaning?" with my heart in it, lead.

Baptist, Catholic, Adventist, I'd seen different doors,
Some words may conflict, yet the message is restored.
The preacher rose, and the floating crowd bowed in a wave,
But I asked, "Where's the mercy you claim you gave?

If free will is genuine, let my questions be heard.
Don't punish a seeker for speaking a word."
Lightning struck hard, yet it left me untouched,
So, I stared in his glow, and I pressed him as such:

"Who are you really?" His mask tore apart
An alien craving worship, not God in his heart.
My wings burst wide, "I'm Gideon," I cried,
"A fighter for Heaven, with truth as my guide."

I cast back the storm; his false power fell,
and I healed the two men he tried to repel.
Then I turned to Mary, voice steady and clear:
"Hold fast for Peter—love like that is rare.
For one short year, I'll teach Christ's living way
Guard Eden, choose good... and rebuild what you can save."
— DTP

A Senator's Past

He came up where the streetlights flicker and fail,
Where hope is a rumor and rent is a rail.
An inner-city kid with a mind like a spark,
Learning to pray with his back to the dark.

He put himself through college late nights, thin meals,
Two jobs, one dream, and a heart made of steel.
While friends chased quick money and praise in the dust,
He chose slow miles because slow miles are just.

But growth has a cost that doesn't show in the suit:
You learn what to cut when you're chasing the fruit.
He loved his people, but some loved the mess
So, he backed up from chaos to build something blessed.

He distanced himself from family, not hate, not pride
Just knowing some ties pull you under the tide.
And he let go of friends with corrupt little plans
Who'd smile in your face with a knife in their hands.

He rose step by step, name by name,
Turned pain into purpose, and pressure to flame.
A scholarship scar and a hustle-made grace,
Now walking the marble with streets in his face.

He spoke for the blocks that get skipped on the map,
For the moms who don't sleep, for the kids in the trap.
He promised the state he would fight for the good
Not just talk like they do… but do what he could.

Yet here's the truth, they don't put on TV:
The past doesn't vanish just cause you're free.
Sometimes it waits like a shadow in the back,
Sometimes it's useful when the wolves attack.

So, when strong arms were needed, when deals got too grim
He had old names he could call, and they'd answer for him.
Not to run dirt, not to break what is right,
But to stand in the doorway and hold back the night.

He kept them at a distance, like tools on a shelf,
A line he wouldn't cross, a test for himself.
Because to do good, you need clean hands, yes
But you also need courage when power comes to the test.

Now glory looks easy from faraway seats,
But it's built in the quiet of tired, stubborn weeks.
A senator's rise isn't gold, it's a bruise
It's losing what you love… so your people can choose.

And if you ask him today what made him that man,
He'll say, "I learned early: you don't rise by chance.
You rise by the choices that hurt but are true
And you carry your city… in all that you do."

— DTP

The Silent Knight: Jay's Undercover Run

In a city where sirens sing low through the night,
Where shadows wear names, and the wrong feels like right,
Two brothers wore badges, but carried a veil
Undercover in chaos, where most men would fail.

Cops and robbers—old stories, same streets, new spin,
They stepped into the game where you don't get to win.
One brother went deep where the daylight can't reach,
In the underworld's mouth, where the monsters don't preach.

And words came back broken, half whisper, half dread:
"He's trapped in the dark… and they want him dead."
So, Jay tightened his coat, kept his face calm and plain,
While his mind drew blueprints like a lock picks a chain.

He moved like a secret, no brag, no display,
just timing, angles, and patience at play.
A smooth-running plan with a razor-edged seam,
Flawless execution, like a well-hidden dream.

He slipped past the lookout, the muscle, the heat,
Past backroom bravado and blood on the street.
With a smile that said nothing, with eyes that saw all,
He walked through their world like a shadow in a hall.

Then a side-door truth hit, small voice, muffled, near:
A missing girl's plea that the night couldn't smear.
Jay paused, not for glory, not for a headline or praise
But because even lions can't stomach that phase.

He flipped the whole script with a quiet command,
Turned fear into footing, put hope in her hand.
Got her out through the cracks that the wicked ignore,
Then he went back for his brother, because that was the core.

Down in the underworld, where the air tastes like rust,
Where deals are made dirty, and trust isn't trust,
Jay found him, bound up in a cold, borrowed room,
two minutes from gone, two inches from doom.

No sirens, no speeches, just method and art:
A distraction, a signal, a key to the heart.
He cut through the danger like silk through a seam,
And pulled his own blood back to safety and his team.
But Jay wasn't finished; he came for the head,
For the kingpin who fed on the lives of the dead.
He laid out the pieces, made every move count,
and turned evidence into an unshakable mount.

Wiretap to Dropbox, a meeting to sting,
A coded little message that broke the whole ring.
The bust of a lifetime, no shots, no parade,
Just the underworld caving to the trap he'd laid.

And when it was over, the city still slept,
Not knowing what darkness, he entered and kept.
No statue, no spotlight, no crown in the light
Just a brother saved, and a girl back home at night.

They asked, "Who did it?" and the answers stayed vague,
like a name whispered softly, then lost in the haze.
Because Jay didn't need fame or a good night,
He vanished like mercy...Jay the silent knight.

— DTP

Destined by Love

Your spirit of love touches me,
The way your eyes look at me, so tender, so true.
This is what I truly miss,
A beauty complete, a woman I kiss.

Your romantic touch is so sweet,
I feel your skin smooth beneath my caress.
From head to toe, my desire is strong.
One day, your heart will come along.

Until that time, though we're apart,
The energy you give has been there from the start.
I feel it when you pass me by,
It lingers, everlasting; it will never die.

As I hold you close, I sense your heart,
I love you completely, never apart.
Closing my eyes, your image appears,
I think of our love through all the years.

Me and you, you and me,
A couple destined, meant to be.
I care for you more than words can say,
Without your love, I lose my way.

As I massage your toes, your energy flows, I
into my hands, a love that knows.
I capture it gently, I hold on tight,
Hoping this feeling never leaves tonight.

My heart knows the truth, clear and pure,
Without you, I can't endure.
Each sigh, each touch, a song of delight,
Our passion burns brightly through the night.

We lose ourselves in a love so deep,
As if the Gods placed it for us to keep. In matrimony,
in passion, in truth, Forever, I give my soul to you.

And as I journey home, my thoughts unwind,
Of how sweet you are, my heart's design.
With every word, with every tone,
I bring you this poem, my love, my own.

— DTP

Lines in the Sand

As I sat upon the beach, I started to ponder,
The waves are crashing, like distant thunder.
My mind was racing, with thoughts galore,
The desire to write, burning like a fire at night.

But alas, I had no paper, no pen in my hand,
Where would I start? How can I make this grand?
A tale that was brewing inside my mind,
A masterpiece waiting to unwind.

But then, as if by fate, I felt my hand hit the sand,
A sign, perhaps, that it was time to take a stand.
To put my thoughts into words, to make them real,
To create something that would make others feel.

So, I took my finger and began to draw,
A line in the sand, a starting point, no flaw.
From there, my thoughts began to flow,
Like the tide that ebbs and flows.

I wrote of love, of loss, of joy and pain,
of life's mysteries that we can't explain.

My finger moved with ease, like a pen on paper.
Each stroke, a word, a memory, a caper.
And as the sun began to set on the horizon,
My poem was complete; my spirits were rising.
With a sense of accomplishment, I gazed upon my creation,
For in that moment, I realized, with elation.

That was all I needed was the sand, the sea,
and my mind unimpeded, to set words free.
To create something beautiful, something real,
to express my thoughts, my heart, my zeal.

And so, as I left the beach that day,
I carried with me a sense of pride, no dismay.
For I knew that no matter where I go,
I could always create poetry with my mind's flow.

— DTP

The Woman of My Dreams

I met you once, or maybe twice,
Or long before that fateful sight,
The moment when my world stood still,
As time itself bent to your will.

You were the woman of my dreams,
Not built from hope or fantasy schemes,
But formed from something profoundly true,
A feeling old, the day I knew.

We walked through years both rough and kind,
Through joy and pain intertwined,
Through laughter loud and nights of tears,
Through growth, through doubt, through passing years.

You loved me when I couldn't see
The man I was supposed to be,
You held a faith I failed to hold,
You warmed my heart when mine grew cold.
I'm sorry that I lost our way,
Some losses whisper, never say
The moment when the end draws near
You only know when it's not here.

If I could turn those days around,
I'd listen more, I'd stand my ground,
I'd love you softer, deeper still,
With hands that heal, with truer will.

Now all I have are words and rhyme,
To keep your love alive in time,
This poem holds what once was real,
A love too deep for time to steal.

You'll always be my sweetest truth,
My borrowed time, my lost-found youth,
The woman of my dreams, my flame,
A love I'll always call by name.
The woman of my dreams!

— DTP

The Knight's Vow

My priority is your happiness,
Provide, Protect, and profess with manliness
My actions will caress your soul.
Your smile has beauty untold,

You are my princess who has turned into a Queen,
and I am the knight of your dreams.
My name, my thoughts, are Chevalier,
A gentleman who truly cares.

Your Ps are noted, and they are my pursuits,
I'll protect you as a knight of the Round Table.
Would defend his Queen.
Provisions provided can be seen,

As I profess my truths to warm your heart.
Your total love will begin to start,
my commitment to you will never wane,
And your commitment to me will be the same.

I imagined unconditional love and all its grandeur.
My, my, my, the love you will endure.
I am true to my word, as you will see.
I'm going to change the three P's.

To the two Ps and an L as requested by the man above:
Where I will Provide, Protect, and Love.

— DTP

Work

I am a team player, through and through,
Working with others is what I do.
I improve my strengths, I listen well,
Communication is key—that much I can tell.

I believe in learning from each day's stride.
In every experience, wisdom will hide.
For your organization's lasting success,
I'm commercially aware, I must confess.

I'll represent your brand with pride,
With care for customers, nothing to hide.
I'll work with purpose, steady and true,
To help achieve the goals set by you.

Above all else, my word I'll keep,
Trustworthy values, loyal and deep.
Integrity guides each choice I make,
every step forward, for your sake.

So, when you're deciding on who to hire,
think of my passion, my drive, my desire.
To join your team, to contribute, and to aspire.
Together, we'll build and climb even higher.

— DTP

Strength in the Fields

Out in the fields of golden wheat,
The Sun beats down in a summer's heat.
I wonder, lost in thought,
Wondering what life has in store, what battles will be fought.

But there's one thing I know, one thing I can say.
I am strong and resilient; I'll make my own way.
With hard work and determination, I'll achieve my goals.
And show the world what I'm made of, and the depths of my soul.

I remember the days when I felt so small,
When the weight of the world would make me fall.
But I got back up, dusted off my knees,
And kept on fighting, despite the disease.

Life can be tough, and the road can be long.
But I will not give up, I will stay strong.
I will face every challenge head-on with a grin,
And emerge victorious, with a heart full of win.

So, if you are feeling lost or down.
Remember that you're strong, with a warrior's crown.
And though the road may be challenging, you can make it through
with hard work, determination, and a heart that is true.

And as the sun sets on another day.
Keep on fighting, come what may.
For I am strong, I am brave,
And I'll keep fighting, to the end of my days.
— DTP

Leadership

In leadership, these virtues we hold dear,
Values we honor and aim to keep clear.
For me, authenticity is my top priority,
A culture of trust and transparency is the key to prosperity.

To be an empathetic leader, I do believe,
One who listens actively and tries to perceive,
The emotions and needs of my team,
Creating a safe space where they can openly dream.

Accountability is another quality I prize,
Taking ownership of mistakes, not hiding behind lies,
Setting clear expectations and following through,
Encouraging my team to do the same, a value so actual.

Vision is essential to guide the way,
To inspire my team to join me and stay,
Communicating effectively, the path we must take,
Aligning with our mission, for everyone's sake.

Lastly, adaptability, the ability to change,
A flexible leader can navigate through the strange,
Challenges may come, and pressures may mount,
But I'll remain calm and help my team surmount.

These are the qualities I hold dear,
As a leader, I'll strive to adhere
To lead with authenticity, empathy, accountability,
Vision and adaptability are a recipe for success
and stability.
— DTP

When We Finally Meet

When we first met, it felt like a dream.
A moment so real, yet surreal it would seem.
From pen to paper, from words to embrace,
at last, I beheld the warmth of your face.

I never imagined what you had become.
Not just a pen pal, but truly the one.
A man who desires a bond so true,
a partner to cherish, a love to pursue.

You are unafraid to let feelings show,
your words touch my heart; they help me to grow.
Sweet morning greetings, poems divine,
each little gesture makes your soul shine.

You speak of the three Ps with a vow.
Provide, protect, profess, and how.
You see me as royalty, your King, your prize,
and I see devotion alive in your eyes.

Yes, time will tell, as it always does,
for love is proven in actions, not buzz.

But with every word, my hope takes flight,
That our future together will blossom bright.

Two hearts united, a bond so rare.
A blissful love we will forever share.
And when we soar, you and me.
I know our love was meant to be.

— DTP

My Heart Remembers You

Oh, how I miss you, where my heart found peace,
where warmth and comfort would never cease.
In my arms, your spirit found rest.
A sacred place where I felt blessed.

If I could turn back the hands of time,
I would relive those moments, so sweet, so prime.
You made me whole, free of all care,
and I was myself simple and bare.

You, my love, such a wondrous being,
I am grateful for every moment of seeing.
That love is pure, a gift so tru.,
My journey feels blessed, all because of you.

Yet here I sit, my heart aching so,
missing your presence, wishing you'd know.
Some moments are gone, left behind,
but they live forever in the heart and mind.

I long for one more day, one more chance,
to say the words, to let love dance.

To give what I left unsaid before
and pour my soul out evermore.

My love for you is steadfast, my Queen.
Only time will reveal the joy it brings.
So, goodnight, my darling, rest in delight,
You are with me, each day and each night.

The words I whispered, it is true,
I was under your spell, enchanted by you.
Saying yes to all, wanting much more,
laughing, alive, with a love I adore.

— DTP

How Do You Feel About Me

As time moves on, our feelings grow,
we teach each other, and show.
My fondness for you has increased, it's true,
Since we first started chatting, I've been falling for you.

I think of you often, I can't deny,
my thoughts of you deepen, and now I know why.
It's a sign of affection, of care so real,
A desire to see you, to share what I feel.

You have many qualities, unique and rare,
A sense of humor, an outgoing flair.
Intelligence, beauty, easy to see,
but most of all, you genuinely care for me.

I can feel love when we talk, it's clear,
Your ethical commitments, I deeply revere.
With every word you say, my worries disappear,
in your honest embrace, I've nothing to fear.

Your values shine bright, like the morning's first light,
Guiding me gently through each lonely night.
Together we flourish, with hearts ever near
I can feel love when we talk; it's clear.

A shared vision of the future means much,
I dream of a life that we can both touch.
I know what you want, and I like it too,
most importantly, my future holds you.

So as time evolves and the days move along,
I want to be with you, that's where I belong.
To grow with you deeply, to love and adore,
And I hope you feel the same.
that's what I'm hoping for.

— DTP

A Plea for Understanding

This note I write with honesty,
A heavy heart yet hope in me.
Please hear these words I humbly send,
A promise to make amends in the end.

My children were picked up with care,
That Friday afternoon was so dear.
But no space remained for me to ride,
a heavy flu kept me inside.

I leaned on family, weak, unwell,
They gave me first aid, as I now tell.
By three o'clock, I made my way,
but I missed my chance to call that day.

I failed to share my troubled state,
Uncertain of her plans, I wait.
Forgive my silence, hesitation.
It came from anger and desperation.

The rent arrears weigh down my soul,
A burden heavy, beyond control.
yet I will strive with all my might
to pay for each coin, o make things right.

I never meant to seem untrue,
Deceit is not the path I choose.
With God's own help, I'll clear the shame,
And mend what's broken in my name.

Your patience and kindness humble me,
A grace so vast, a gift so free.
I pray the Lord will bless your days,
And crown your life with joy and praise.

Together we'll find a fair solution,
with open hearts and resolution.
I'll meet with you, we'll plan, discuss,
and forge a way that honors us.

So, thank you for the love you've shown,
for standing by when hope felt gone.
I vow to do what must be done,
to pay in full—until it's won.

— DTP

Rich in My Dreams

I dreamt I was a sailor on the ocean deep,
Sailing around the world while others sleep.
I played draw poker as we left the land
I won a million dollars on the very first hand.

I played and played until the crew was broke.
I was king at poker; I was no joke.
I won every bet, every hand I drew,
Couldn't lose a dollar if I wanted to.

I docked in Siam, and I laughed, half-mean,
"Where in the hell am I?" some far-off scene.
I played the king, and I won a million more.
I had to leave the island because the king got sore.

I went to Monte Carlo to play roulette
I couldn't lose a penny, and I won every bet.
Played the roulette wheels, and I made them sing.
I won every penny like I owned the thing.

I played and played until the bank went broke
I was king at poker; I was no joke.
Chips stacked high like a tower of gold,
And not one cold loss did my hands ever hold.

I searched for a table, a new place to be,
And drifted to Dubai by the shimmering sea.
I couldn't lose a penny, don't ask me why,
Luck sat on my shoulder and winked at the sky.

I played and played till Dubai went broke.
I couldn't lose a penny; I was no joke.
So off to Hong Kong with lights by the shore.
Where the cards hit the table, lose, win, or draw.

I played Mata Hari till she couldn't stay,
I won a million dollars, and I sailed away.
I had to leave that island, couldn't stay anymore,
Cause everywhere I landed… I won a million more.

I'm rich in my dreams, yeah, rich as can be
Then I woke up laughing… dressed to a tee.
— DTP

Happy Valentine's Day

My fireplace, so warm and so bright,
A symbol of love, in the twilight
The flames dance in a gentle embrace,
Of two hearts, tango-like Salsa's grace.

Like the fire, our love will glow,
With each kiss, it continues to grow.
In your arms, you feel complete,
Together, we'll weather any heat.

The room is quiet, but our hearts sing,
With each moment, our love spread like wings.
With each ember, our love will flourish,
A bond that we will always nourish.

We'll sit together, by the fire's light,
bask in love's warm and gentle sight.
Like the flames, our love will soar,
Our passion will scorch heaven's door

So let us hold hands and watch the fire,
As it dances, a love that will never tire.
So Happy Valentine's Day, my love,
To the one sent from heaven above.

With you, my heart is warm and bright,
Forever and always, meant to be, tonight.
In my arms, you feel safe,
Your love for me will always be the case.

Like the fire, our love will burn,
A love that will always return.
So let us gaze into the fire
And look into each other's eyes.

With each moment, our love will rise,
Happy Valentine's Day, my dear,
To the one who makes my heart sing with cheer.

— DTP

The Gift

Good news, I heard today,
I'm going golfing with President Obama, they say.
My Secret Santa left me the best gift ever,
an elegant cherry Cedarwood case that will last forever.

Inside, a three-piece golf club set to impress,
made with such care, no detail to guess.
Two top-flight golf balls, titanium steel,
with tracking inside, they'll never conceal.

No matter how dense the foliage may be,
these balls will be waiting, easy to see.
The Cedarwood club is a sight to behold,
with laser pointers to guide every putt, as told.

Topping it off, a treasure so rare,
an official signature, penned with care.
From President Obama, a keepsake so fine,
A gift I'll cherish for all of time.

Grateful I am for this wondrous splendor,
Thanks to the kindness of Dr. Periandor.
But one question remains, exciting and true
Which golf course will we do?

I hope to impress with my skills on the green,
To show President Obama what golfing can mean.
"FORE-CADDIE!" I'll shout with a voice full of cheer,
As I play every stroke with a joy that's sincere.

I'll give my best to make each shot proud,
Stand with honor, my heart avowed.
And when the game is over, I'll head back home,
to display this gift on a mantelpiece dome.

— DTP

Wheat

Out in the fields of golden wheat,
the sun beats down in summer's heat,
I wonder, lost in thought,
Wondering what life has in store, what battles will be fought.

But there's one thing I know, one thing I can say,
I am strong and resilient; I'll make my own way.
With hard work and determination, I'll achieve my goals
and show the world what I'm made of and the depths of my soul.

I remember the days when I felt so small,
when the weight of the world would make me fall.
I got back up, dusted off my knees,
and kept on fighting, despite the disease.

For life can be tough, and the road can be long,
I won't give up, I'll stay strong.
I'll face every challenge, head-on with a grin,
and emerge victorious, with a heart full of win.

So, if you're feeling lost or down,
remember that you're strong, with a warrior's crown.

Though the road may be challenging, you can make it through
with hard work, determination, and a heart that's true.

And as the sun sets on another day,
I'll keep on fighting, come what may.
I am strong, I am brave.
I'll keep on fighting to the end of my days.
— DTP

A New Day

With each new dawn, I sigh and rise.
Dust off my feet and look up to the skies.
The sun's rays bring new hope and light.
Dispelling my gloom with all their might

When clouds are dark, my heart is sad
I dance in the rain; it makes me glad.
Washing away my tears and fears,
leaving my soul feeling fresh and clear

As evening falls, I count my blessings.
Grateful for the strength to keep on pressing.
Life is a mystery, but we can make it beautiful.
By being dutiful, merciful, and bountiful.

May your tomorrow bring good tidings.
And each new day is full of blessings.
Thank you for your love and support.
For in my battles, you are my fort.

With full armor on and God on my side
I face each challenge with a heart full of pride.
Jehovah Rapha is the true healer, I trust.

And in His love and grace, I know I must.

Thank you for being my rock and guide.
With you by my side, I never have to hide.
Good morning, beautiful. I love you more each day.
May your day be blessed in every way.

— DTP

Rise from the ashes like the phoenix!

Apart

Although a thousand miles stretch wide,
In your gaze, my body is still deeply tied.
Distance tries to play its worldly part,
But our love's a flame, à la carte of the heart.

Through valleys and hills, o'er mountains high,
Our love flows like fountains to the sky.
In your eyes, a brand-new life to start.
Here's looking at you, kid, like Bogart.

No matter how great the miles may be,
love unites us, strong and free.
In your eyes, constellations play their part,
guiding through the night, never to depart.

Though oceans may roar, and worlds may spread,
In your eyes, I find where my love is led.
Hand in hand, our tale's a work of art,
In your embrace, we're never torn apart.

With love as our compass, we'll find our way,
On this chart of life, we'll dance and sway.

A thousand miles may seem a remarkable feat,
but love knows no bounds, when our hearts meet.

— DTP

Confession in the Moonlight

In the story of our words, a tale unfolds,
A conversation of uncertainty, it holds.
"What were you thinking?" you asked,
A mind with a question that's unmasked

You said, "What comes next?"
But in that uncertain moment, I was vexed.
I found my errors and mended my ways,
I asked for forgiveness in the coming days.

For if it's a happy ever after, we will share,
I'll find joy in whatever we both dare.
Our words, like poems, in this moment unite,
a confession of love, in the moonlight.

You've asked questions, and here are my replies,
As we journey through life, beneath the boundless skies.
Something that gives me butterflies, it's true,
When I profess my love to you.

What were you thinking, you inquired today,
I'd say it's the passion in my eyes; I'd convey.
In the silence of my thoughts, unspoken words reside,
All I wanted to say, in my heart, I've tried to hide.

But now, the time has come to let my feelings flow,
To express the love and emotions I've held below.
And in the oddest of places, a memory stirs,
The most inconvenient moment recurs.

A doubt unfounded by missing information,
worried about religious creation.
A spark ignited, like a hidden flame,
in the depths of our souls, it came.

In the garden of my heart, a bloom so rare,
I must confess the love I cannot help but bear.
Your smile, a radiant sunbeam in my day,
your laughter, a melody that sweeps me away.

In your presence, I find peace and grace,
a love so profound, it's an endless embrace.
I cherish every moment, every word we share, for
in your love, I find love so rare.

So here I stand, my heart laid bare,

to profess my love, to show you I genuinely care.

— DTP

Hollow Remains

I misplaced my soul in the silence of the night,
Where shadows dissolved what once felt right.
The echo of purpose has faded away,
A ghost of ambition with nothing to say.

The desk stands empty, the work is undone,
my job was a battle, already lost and won.
Now the hours are hollow, long and bare,
with nothing to build and no one to care.

Hope was a lantern I carried with pride,
but its flame has gone dark, no spark left inside.
I wander through days like a stranger unknown,
A shell of a man, and a heart made of stone.

If the soul can return, if the spark can re-ignite,
then guide me from sorrow back into the light.
But until that dawn, I am fractured, un-whole.
A body still breathing, a man without a soul.

— DTP

Kindling the Dawn

I thought my soul was shattered, gone,
but even at night, the sky waits for dawn.
The silence that weighed so heavily before.
Now whispers of pathways, of something more.

A love lost was not the end,
but a chapter that bends, a road that can mend.
For the purpose is larger than the titles we bear,
It lives in love and the moments we share.

Hope rekindles in the smallest flame.
A stranger's smile, a gentle name.
Though darkness lingers, I've come to see,
the spark I need still lives in me.

When I rise, though broken and scarred,
I'll carry the strength of battles hard.
For even a soul, once lost, can be found,
In hope's quiet voice, where grace still resounds.

— DTP

In the Colors of Love

How do I feel when your hand finds mine?
Like walls that fall away and like stars that realign.
The world may still whisper, but love speaks clearly,
A bond beyond measure, unbroken, sincerely.

Yes, there are moments when the stares linger long,
questions unspoken of right, or of wrong.
But in your embrace, their noise drifts away,
your heartbeat assures me we'll find our own way.

Your skin and my skin, two shades, one flame,
no border, no boundary, no need for a name.
Each kiss is a promise; each touch is a vow;
The world may divide, but it cannot stop now.

For love is not written in color or race,
it blooms in the soul; it's the warmth we embrace.
How do I feel? Both fragile and strong,
tested by trials yet pulled by a song.

A song that reminds us, though different we seem,
together we're living a radiant dream.
And so, we keep walking, hearts beating as one,
our story is not ending, it's only begun.

—DTP

What Do I Want?

Do I want money, the glitter of gold,
treasures and riches, possessions untold?
They dazzle the eye, but fade in the night,
A hollowed-out victory, gone with the light.

Do I want riches, power, and fame,
A legacy carved by fortune's name.
Yet crowns can grow heavy, and jewels won't decay,
Their shine doesn't keep the loneliness away.

What I want truly is simple, profound,
companionship's warmth where the heart is found.
A hand to hold through life's shifting tide,
A love everlasting, with you by my side.

For wealth may crumble and riches depart,
but love is the gold that enriches the heart.
So, what do I want? It is clear, it is true:
Not the world's treasures, only you.

— DTP

I See You

I see you.
The love in your eyes.
The longing in your heart,
the quiet hunger hidden in your gaze.

I see your wants,
your secret desires.
The whispers of passion you try not to say.

And everything you seek,
everything you dream,
I shall give it to you

like a genie in a bottle,
Bound only to your wish,
set free by your touch.

For in your eyes I find my purpose, in your heart,
I find my home, and in your desires,

I find the fire
that makes us whole.

— DTP

The Second Half

The second half of life unfolds like a dream,
work behind us, yet joy in the stream.
The world spreads wide, a canvas anew,
painted with moments of me and you.

We wander through Italy, streets lined with song,
Where passion and history carry us along.
On a soothing island, Saint Lucia's embrace,
The sea whispers love in a tender place.

A stay in Dubai, where the skyline glows,
Deserts of gold and mystery it shows.
Then sails on the ocean, the stars overhead,
Romance in waves, by the moonlight we're led.

The aurora borealis, a dream in the sky,
Colors like prayers that shimmer and fly.
Each bucket-list wonder, a treasure to see,
yet no one shines as bright as your love next to me.

For the journeys, the travels, and the sights all around,
they're sweeter because it's your hand I've found.
The second half of life is more than just new.
It's living in the world while exploring you.

— DTP

Lovely Bride

You stand in front of the mirror, doubting the glass.
Tracing the shadows that flicker and pass.
You ask what I see when I look your way.
My answer is simple, yet hard to say.

For the mirror shows lines, the years that have grown,
But my heart sees a beauty that's always been known.
No jewel can compare, no star in the skies,
to the light that forever shines in your eyes.

Roses may blossom, diamonds may gleam,
But none hold the glow of the love that I've seen.
The ocean, the sunset, the morning's first light,
all fade when I hold you close in the night.

You are lovely, my darling, beyond what is shown.
A wonder, a treasure that's only my own.
Though mirrors may falter, their vision is untrue.
All I will ever see is the beauty in you.

My joyous, wonderful, lovely bride
Who casts a reflection of beauty when my eyes open wide.

— DTP

Beyond Pigment

What shade we wear, what creed we claim,
What wealth we hold, what honored name
These things are fleeting; they fade with the years,
But the heart still hungers, the soul still hears.

For we are all human, with needs that are true,
A longing for love, for someone, for you.
So, forgo tradition, let old walls fall,
forget about pigment; it doesn't matter at all.

If you love, then love deeply, with all your flame,
If you admire, admire with no hint of shame.
Be true to yourself, let your spirit be free,
Take a chance on the wonders of what love could be.

Explore every color, each shade of the skin,
For love has no border, it blossoms from within.
You may find a treasure, a gift unforeseen.
A love that's more vivid than any dream.

So, carpe diem, lascia che L'amore sia raccontato.
Let happiness guide you, let new stories unfold.

For myths melt away when the heart sees what's true:

The beauty of life may be waiting for you.

— DTP

The greatest Love

Years ago, I met a rare flower,
An Asian bloom beyond compare.
Her presence lit the world I knew,
fierce passion wrapped in gentleness, too.

The wonder, the joy, the feelings we found,
Were treasures that bloomed, profound and unbound.
Like tasting sugar for the very first time,
Sweeter than sweet, in rhythm and rhyme.

This love touched my soul, deep and true,
Surpassing fascination, reshaping all I knew.
Not just desire, not fleeting delight,
But a love so eternal, it felt wholly right.

Though we parted, her spirit remains.
A whisper of joy, a sweet refrain.
I feel her beside me, despite all these years,
Her memory comforts me through laughter and tears.

For love such as ours cannot fade or decay,
It lingers forever; it lights up my way.

I pray for one glance, for destiny's call

To meet the greatest love of all.

— DTP

A Garden of the Loves I Miss

I miss you as the roses miss
the warmth of the morning sun.
Their crimson hearts remember
the days when love was young.

I miss you as the lilies miss the
whisper of the breeze,
those gentle winds that carried hope
across their ivory seas.

I miss you as the tulips miss the
first soft touch of spring,
a burst of color, brief and bright,
a fragile, precious thing.

I miss you as the orchids miss a
careful, tender hand,
exotic blooms that only thrive,
when someone understands.

I miss you as carnations miss
the vows they used to bear,
still holding on to whispered dreams,
that lingered in the air.

I miss you as the jasmine misses
Moonlight's silver glow.
A fragrance drifting through the night,
to places only lovers know.

I miss you as the violets miss
a voice to call them home.
Small blossoms craving company
when left to stand alone.

My heart has grown into a garden now,
each flower marked by you.
A field of longing, soft and vast,
where love still pushes through.
And though we stand on separate paths,
my soul knows this is true:
Every bloom that aches for light still
turns its face to you.

Keep Hope Alive

The dreams we hold, the tales we weave,
are seeds of hope that we believe.
Each story told, each vision bright,
becomes a lantern in night.

You hope for love, a gentle wife,
you hope for joy, a better life.
You hope the path will turn out right
and guide you safely through the night.

Yet destiny, with unseen streams,
It is written softly in our dreams.
A tapestry of what must be,
woven with threads of hope set free.

Hope is a treasure, tender and true,
A gift of the heart that carries you through.
So, take it with you in all that you do
I hope for your joy, and good days too.

Keep hope alive, let it never fade,
it builds the future our spirits have made.
For in every hope, a dream takes flight,
A beacon of love, a promising light.

Dreams we carry, stories we tell,
shape the life we know so well.
Hope for love, for joy, for light,
hope- will guide your steps through the night.

Destiny's written in dreams we weave,
In every hope, we choose to believe.
So, hold it close, let your spirit thrive,
always, always, keep hope alive

— **DTP**

I Will Not Fall

I will not fall to life's cruel woes,
No matter the storms the future shows.
When trials rise, and shadows call,
I'll stand my ground; I will not fall.

When the road is hard, and the climb is steep,
I dig in deeper, my fire runs deep.
Redoubling efforts, I push through the night,
for dreams are worth the fiercest fight.

If I stumble, I rise again,
for falling is never the true end.
Life's not measured by each hard hit,
but by the will that refuses to quit.

You only lose when you stop the climb,
when you silence the hope that once was mine.
For every "no" hides a chance to ask,
A door unopened, a waiting task.

So, hear my vow, both strong and tall:
I will not yield. I will not fall!

— DTP

Gods hand

When I cannot help myself,
When prayers sit silent on the shelf,
the Lord sends love through those who care,
A hand to hold, a whispered prayer.

Support lifts me when I am weak,
God's grace shines through the ones I seek.
Brothers and sisters, hear his call,
be the strength that breaks my fall.

To give support is Heaven's way,
A blessing shared from day to day.
To receive is humbling, pure, and kind,
A touch of Christ, in heart and mind.

For we are told to serve, to stand,
To lift each other hand in hand.
And when you ask, "Lord, where are You?"
He answers softly: "I'm in the ones who carry you."
So, do you need a hand today?
I'll pray with you; I'll walk your way.
Together in faith, both strong and true,
with God beside us, there's nothing we can't do.

— DTP

A Love I Pray to Keep

I sit here wondering what life will hold,
How can we see the future before we grow old?
Tell us, dear God, how can it be,
Why do our hearts keep loving so freely?

We pray she won't fade to a memory of love,
but live in our soul, a gift from above.
The things we fear most are the first to be lost,
Please, Lord, don't let this be love's high cost.

Our heart sinks each time we think of her face,
Her love came upon us with a sudden embrace.
We'll never feel whole, nor truly completed,
Without her by our side, our life feels defeated.

For some, losing time is knowing what is gone,
but we don't want that lesson—we've known it too long.
What can we do to amend our mistake?
Our hearts are still aching, it trembles, it breaks.

God, we love her—we'll never deny,
Each thought of her leaving still makes us cry.
Relationships blossom; they're destined to be,
and all that we wish is for marriage to be.

We need her. We'll give her the love we can show.
We'll cherish her deeply; we want her to know.
We sense that she feels it; her heart speaks it too.
But tell me, dear Lord, what more can we do?

This love is much greater than us,
Please guide us, O Lord, to rebuild her trust.

— DTP

Eruption of Desire

The fire within my belly and heart,
rages like a volcano, tearing the earth apart.
Love is natural, a timeless thing,
yet none so fierce as a volcano's sting.

Should it be passion that drives me clear,
or is it the feeling that I fear?
Of the two, neither is so grand or rare,
I cannot adapt to loving her there.

My inspiration is but a passion, you see,
A fancy desire, a burning in me.
Libido crashing, yet rising above,
only inspired by her endless love.

— DTP

To make you sigh

My darling, though you're feeling weak today,
I'll chase the clouds and sweep the sickness away.
If love could heal, I'd send it too,
A thousand roses just for you.

The fire inside me burns so bright,
It warms your heart through the darkest night.
Your smile's the sun, your eyes the sea,
The world is perfect when you're with me.

If I could, I'd whisper low,
Like Rudolph Valentino in a midnight show.
A single glance, a tender sigh,
I'd hold your hand and never ask why.

So, rest, my love, let worries part,
I'll guard your dreams and protect your heart.
For every beat my chest has known,
It longs for you, for you alone.

And when you rise, refreshed, anew,
I'll paint the skies in shades of you.
For love this grand was heaven-sent,
A gift of fate, a sweet descent.

Call my name, and I'll be near,
To chase away your every fear.
For I would cross both time and space,
Just to see the smile upon your face.

Fall in love, don't turn away,
This heart is yours—forever to stay.
For nothing greater can there be
than my love, entwined within me.

— DTP

Dear John

Dearest John, this gift is for you,
To hold your dreams, both old and new.
A place to write, to let them stay,
And guide your heart along the way.

I'll help you read them, hand in hand,
Together we'll learn, together we'll stand.
Without your laughter, the world feels cold,
No jokes, no "wow," no joy to hold.

I miss your smile, your gentle glow,
More than these simple words can show.
But seeing you now, my heart takes flight,
you make the day feel warm and bright.

So, keep this gift, and think of me,
For love like ours was meant to be.

—AC DTP

The Auction of Shadows

I dreamt I wandered through the night,
An auction house beneath dim light.
To buy her a brush to keep,
An electric gift from a sale so cheap.

The auctioneer there smiled, his voice was grim,
"Parents auction off their kin.
Their children's toys, their loved ones' things,
For money's sake, the gavel rings."

I said I'd come at morning's call,
First thing at dawn, I'd take it all.
A toothbrush bright, some toys in hand,
for a toddler lost in a shadowed land.

But soon I felt a chilling change,
The items seemed so dark, so strange.
"These are not mine," I softly pled,
The auctioneer just bowed his head.

"When loved ones die, their things are sold,
Unopened boxes, treasures of old.
The bargains come at a ghostly price,
But silence keeps the sale precise."

I cried, "Why not say this before?"
He laughed, "You'd never buy them, I'm sure.
All sales are final, the deal is done,
No refunds here, for anyone."

The sky grew twisted, the air grew thin,
A haunted howl crept deep within.
I started to float, my body unwound,
The auctioneer shouted,
"The toys and brush—ghosts, put him down!"

I trembled, I gasped, my heart nearly broke,
I whispered, "Whoa," then I awoke.
I ran from the house, the estate grew small,
The sunset blazed, and I outran it all.

And thinking back, through fear and fright,
I laughed alone in the dead of night.

—DTP

The Estate of Night (Ode to E.A. Poe)

I dreamt I went to an auction
To purchase, in some strange devotion,
An electric brush, a simple thing,
Yet dread did coil, its shadow cling.

The keeper spoke with a voice so hollow,
"Parents here their fate must follow.
They auction children, loved ones too,
That strangers' dreams renew."

I answered, "Sir, at morning's chime,
I shall return and spend my Dime.
A brush I'll claim, and toys besides,
For toddler hands so satisfied."

Yet soon a chill did o'er me creep,
The air grew heavy, dark, and deep. "These
things are not mine—sir, they are wrong."
He whispered low, "You've known all along.

"When loved ones die, their goods are laid
in boxes sealed, in silence stayed.
At auction sold at bargain's breath,
For coin is dearer here than death."

I cried, "Why not confess before?
I'd never buy at such a haunted store!"
He smirked and said, "No sale, no pay
All sales are final, night or day."

The sky grew torn, the heavens bled,
The earth quaked beneath my tread.
I floated high in ghostly thrall,
Till toys and brush obeyed his call.

"Put him down," the auctioneer cried,
Their voices were cold, as if they'd died.
I fell in terror, gasped in fright,
And woke beneath the fading light.

I ran, I fled, the sunset glared,
The estate behind me shrank and stared.
Yet in my chest, through fear and blight,
I laughed alone at death's grim sight.

—DTP

Paradise by the Sea

I see the wave rippling towards land,
It roars on the beach like a well-played band.
A sound so sweet, so pure, so clear,
No worry, no burden, nothing to fear.

Paradise is where we all belong,
Where exotic birds lift hearts in song.
I look around and wonder this:
If heaven is here, it's not to be missed.

Night descends, the stars ignite,
Painting the sky with colors so bright.
Paradise, a vision rare,
A dream fulfilled beyond compare.

These vivid images will never flee,
Etched in my soul by that wonderful sea.
Shooting stars race across the night,
I wonder about their journey, their secret flight.

I sit on the beach, drink in hand,
My fingers are sifting through warm, soft sand.
Each grain that slips, so small, so slight,
becomes a star that graces the night.

I think of times that came before,
And gaze to heaven, longing for more.
Waves still crash, the breezes teach,
As I sip my Mai Tai along the beach...

It makes me wonder where I've been,
and dream of what I've seen.

— DTP

Dream of Us

Upon a beach, secluded, still,
The moonlight cast its silver will.
The waves, they sang their endless song,
A world where only we belong.

The night was warm, the breeze was near,
It brushed our skin, it drew us near.
Your presence wrapped me, soft, divine,
yet distance lingered, sharp as a line.

I leaned in closely, my breath touched your skin,
A trembling shiver stirred within.
My lips brushed lightly, a fleeting flame,
And all the world was not the same.

Your softness lingered, tasted so sweet,
My heart drummed wild, a frantic beat.
Our mouths then met, our tongues entwined,
A rhythm only ours to find.

A kiss of fire, of souls combined,
The world erased, no ties confined.
Your eyes met mine, love's endless stream,
Two souls now bound within a dream.

The beach, the waves, the night grew dim,
our hearts beat strong in a perfect hymn.
Desire burned, yet soft, yet deep,
A love too vast for words to keep.

Then morning came, the dream was gone,
I woke up to find myself alone.
Sadness lingered, but hope took flight,
For love like this, I must one day write.

That dream is truth, reality,
Your soul, your body, one with me.
Our hearts as one, forever near,
A love eternal, pure and sincere.

— DTP

Lightning's Gift

In the dream, a storm rolled in, black, wide, and loud,
And one lone soul stood steady under the cloud.
Lightning struck, white fire, a split of sky
Yet they didn't burn... they rose, eyes lifted high.

Then came the knowing: infinite and clear
Every language spoken as it lived in their ear.
All history was revealed from the planet's first day,
and secrets lost to fallen worlds found their way.

They named the ruins buried under the sea,
The books burned down, the truths we couldn't see.
They showed us how old empires learned to fall
Not one big crash... but pride that poisoned all.

So, they stitched us together, enemy to friend,
Turning borders into bridges, watching wounds mend.
They healed the land, cooled the fevered sky,
and taught the world to live... before it died.

And as the thunder softened into the night,
They whispered, "Knowledge is the light and love makes it right."

— DTP

Free Will

God gave us free will to control our fate,
Hopefully, we act before it's too late.
When fortune fades, and spirits feel slight,
The first thing you think of is to pray through the night.

You plead for doors to finally swing wide,
For blessings and hope to stay by your side.
You check the mail, hoping for a sign,
Praying today will be better than mine.

But remember when your heart grows still,
God has gifted us free will.
If you don't ask, the answer is "no,"
But if you move forward, the path will show.

So be kind to all the souls you meet, for
life is brief, and fate is discreet.
Free will is easy to claim with pride,
But it's harder to live when it's tested inside.

Free will, free will, a gift so true,
A power God planted in me and you.
In despair, when shadows cling tight,
It guides us forward; it sparks the light.

Free will lets you rise and choose your way,
To shape your tomorrow from the trials of today.
It shapes your destiny, bold and free,
Molding you into the soul you're destined to be.

— DTP

Ghost in the Cabinet

I walked out of the house from a last will's ink,
Still trying to piece together what others think.
"Uncle Phil is gone," the papers had said.
So why did the place feel like someone wasn't dead?

I toured the rooms with a cautious grin,
Wondering if moving in would feel like sin.
Dust on the windows, silence so thick.
Until the cupboard latch snapped...click... click.

The door swung open like it had a plan,
And I froze mid-step like a startled man.
"Alright," I muttered, "who's playing games?"
The house stayed quiet; it didn't name names.

So, I went full hero, bold and loud,
Ready to chase that spirit out of the crowd.
I set up traps, I sprinkled salt,
I talked real tough like I was built like a vault.

I laid down lines, I checked each latch,
I tried every trick from a haunted match.

But nothing worked, no net, no snare,
Just that cabinet breathing in the air.

Then I got tired of all my pride,
And spoke plain truth with no place to hide:
"Look… just get out. I'm not here to fight."
A voice said, "Okay." …like that was alright.

I blinked and laughed at how simple it went.
"If I knew that, I'd have asked where you went!"
And that's when the whisper turned warm and real,
Like family talking behind the veil:

"Nephew," it said, "don't look so shocked.
It's Uncle Phil… and I've been unlocked.
Not to scare you, not to play.
I couldn't leave 'til I showed the way."

The cabinet creaked, then swung wide as a stage,
And behind the boards, like a hidden page
A vault, a map, a tucked-in deed,
And a number too wild for a man to read:

Three hundred million, left in my name,
Not a rumor, not a joke, not a greedy game.
My knees went weak, my heartbeat fast
A ghostly blessing from the past.

And it's weird, the twist of it all:
Most folks see ghosts, and their courage falls.
But there I stood, smiling instead.
Happy to meet my uncle, they told me he was dead.

Cause usually I'd be scared to death, no lie,
but family shows up... and fear walks by.
Go figure, life's strange, dreams too, it seems:
I got rich off a ghost... in my kitchen cabinets' dreams.

— DTP

In The Dream

In a slumber, where silence flows,
A vision stirred, the dream light glows.
She lay beside me, soft and fair.
In the dream... in the dream, I found her there.

I drew her close, her breath so deep,
A tender rhythm, hushed in sleep.
Desire burned, a blazing flame
In the dream... in the dream, I called her name.

She whispered low, her voice so true, "
I love you, "words my spirit knew.
"Don't stop," she sighed, with love sincere,
In the dream... in the dream, I held her near.

No chain of time, no earthly scheme,
Could break the bond we forged in the dream.
Our hearts as one, beyond despair
In the dream... in the dream, I found her there.

— DTP

ACKNOWLEDGMENT

To my dear friend, Anny,

Thank you for your insight and quiet genius in recognizing that dreams and passing thoughts should be captured for later reflection. You were the one who reminded me that what slips through the mind at night can become something meaningful in the light of day.

Because of you, I began writing down these dreams and realized they deserved to be shared. What started as fragments of memory became poems and stories that, I hope, make for rich and thoughtful reading. Your belief that my inner world was worth recording helped bring this collection to life, and for that I am deeply grateful.

NOTES ON SELECTED POEMS

"The Auction of Shadows"

This poem was born from a dream that began as something semi-scary, the kind of nightmare every child knows—the feeling of being chased by something you can't quite see. Yet, as I woke up, the fear shifted into something almost humorous. I realized that even our darkest dreams can lose their power once we step back into waking life. "The Auction of Shadows" captures that transformation: from terror to laughter, from running away to standing up and walking out of the dream on my own terms. It is a reminder that sometimes monsters are made of smoke, and we have more power than we think.

"Ode to E. A. Poe"

The same dream that inspired "The Auction of Shadows" led me to reflect on Edgar Allan Poe. I have always felt that Poe had a passion for words and a rare ability to manipulate language like music— haunting, rhythmic, and unforgettable. He is, by far, one of my favorite poets and storytellers, capturing frightening scenes and eerie moods with such vivid clarity that you feel them in your bones. "Ode to E. A. Poe" is my tribute to that craft: a salute to a master who showed me how darkness, when handled with skill, can become art that lingers long after the last line.

"The Woman of My Dreams"

The Woman of My Dreams came from a rare lightning-strike moment, meeting someone for the first time and instantly knowing she caught your heart. She was a native of Guyana, beautiful in that effortless way an island girl carries herself, like sunshine and saltwater following her everywhere. I tried more than once to take her out, hoping to turn that first spark into something tangible, but she didn't accept because she had to return home. The poem holds that mix of wonder and disappointment, the sweetness of meeting someone unforgettable, and the ache of realizing some connections are meant to be felt, remembered, and released like a tide pulling back to sea.

ABOUT THE AUTHOR – DEMETRIUS "THE POET AND DREAM MASTER"

The name "The Poet and Dream Master" was given to me because of my vivid imagination and the way my dreams spill over into my writing. I have always been drawn to poetry. As a child, I listened to a radio host who recited powerful poems on the air, and those words stayed with me.

In school, I was once selected to write a poem, even though I had no idea where to begin. Around that time, I heard a radio personality perform a poem with such feeling that it lit a spark inside me. That moment is when the poet in me was born.

The title "Dream Master" came later, after I began sharing my dreams with friends. As I discussed these experiences, whether unusual, humorous, or unsettling, it became evident that dreams serve not merely as occurrences but also as valuable sources for literary creation, such as stories and poems.

Over time, the nickname stuck, and it now feels like a true reflection of who I am: a man who walks between waking life and the dream world, gathering words from both.

MY JOURNEY AND FUTURE WORKS

My journey as an author is only beginning, but it has been a long time in the making. I started as a curious kid, fueled by imagination and a quiet sense that there was more to the world than what we see on the surface. Over the years, life, work, family, faith, and countless late-night thoughts have all fed into the voice you hear in these pages.

This collection is the first volume in a two-part poetry series, and I am already at work on Volume 2. The themes of dreams, love, struggle, faith, and transformation will continue to unfold as I explore new corners of the mind and heart.

Beyond poetry, I am also developing a book titled ***The King's Descendant: Rise to Power***, a fascinating journey through time and space that follows a child driven by curiosity and quiet genius. It is a story about legacy, identity, and the unseen forces that shape who we become.

There are more books in progress—more dreams to translate into words, more thoughts to share with readers who see themselves in these lines. These are fascinating times for me as a new author, and I am grateful to everyone who chooses to walk this path with me, page by page and dream by dream.

www.ingramcontent.com/pod-product-compliance
Lightning Source LLC
Chambersburg PA
CBHW040925190426
43197CB00033B/102